Ivies

HAZEL KEY

LONDON
The Royal Horticultural Society
Revised 1981

Contents

Illustrations from Harry Smith Horticultural Photographic Collection

1. Introduction

Ivy *(Hedera)* belongs to the family Araliaceae and contains only a small number of separate species. The cultivars within the species are numerous, particularly in *Hedera helix*. *Hedera* is the old Latin name for ivy and is the name used botanically, but in Britain in everyday language, ivy is the most common name. It is an ornamental, woody shrub cultivated as a handsome hardy evergreen climber. The plant's normal habit is to climb upwards where the stems attach themselves by means of short stem suckers to suitable supports such as tree trunks, walls and posts. When trailing downwards it will grow quite happily without attachment to any object. When growing as ground cover it puts out long roots at, and sometimes a little below, its joints which as real roots are distinct from the suckers on the stem. The leaves come in many forms, crenate, dentate, entire, lobed, serrate or undulate, and the leaf colouring ranges through many shades of green, bronze, black, purple, yellow, green and yellow and green and white variegated; the variegation appears as blotching, spotting or marbling. When blooms appear they are green or yellow, in umbels arranged in terminal panicles*. The fruits are black or yellow with three to five seeds, and when about to flower for the first time, the plant undergoes a great permanent transformation. Starting in the spring of the year in which the plant is going to flower, a few shoots that will bear the first blooms high up on the plant begin to change form. The new leaves do not have points and take on an ovate shape. The stem thickens and grows away from its support. Gradually continuing downwards the leaves all over the plant will alter and the ends of the stems will no longer cling but will grow outwards like branches. It usually takes a year or more to do this but when this process has finished the plant will always grow in this form and continues to flower and fruit each year. The leaves on these shrubs are now called "adult" as distinct from the previous form which is known as "juvenile". Cuttings taken from the adult form take longer to root and the plants grown from these are known as arborescent or tree ivies. They do not revert to the juvenile stage, but grow with a thick-stemmed bushy habit and do not produce any trails.

At this point a brief mention of the two distinct forms of growth produced by the *Hedera* species might be worthwhile. It is normal for *Hedera* to pass through a phase of juvenile growth before reaching the adult form (the latter being known as *arborescent* growth) and there are a number of differences between the two forms, summed up in the table overleaf:

*An *umbel* describes the arrangement of a flower in which all the individual flower stalks arise from the same point.
A *panicle* is a large branched flower cluster, each with many individually stalked flowers.

	Juvenile	Adult
1.	Lobed leaf	Generally unlobed, or very slightly lobed leaf.
2.	No flowers produced.	Flowers and then fruits produced.
3.	Climbing or creeping, with many aerial roots or suckers.	Arborescent form with no aerial roots.
4.	Leaves arranged in one plane on the stem.	Leaves arranged spirally round the stem.

Fig. 1. Hedera in its juvenile form.

It is generally thought that this metamorphosis is essentially a condition produced in response to external stimuli, but the response has been too little studied for it to be completely explained. As far as is known

Fig. 2. Hedera in its arborescent form.

there is no specific period of time that has to elapse before the plant reaches maturity.

Many ivies remain in a juvenile stage for years either because the environmental conditions in which they are growing are not conducive to maturity, they are not old enough, or they are not growing upwards. It is easiest to observe this phenomenon in the wild, where it can be seen that all the flowering or fruiting ivies grow on the perimeter of a wood or on the edges of pathways or clearings within the wood. The ivy growing up a tree in the densely wooded parts retains the juvenile form as does the ivy growing along the ground although even they will sometimes produce adult growth. Ivy looks rather untidy when growing as wall adornment and allowed to mature and flower, and for this reason regular clipping is recommended, so that it will tend to keep its juvenile form. The adult form looks rather splendid when it is growing up a tree. Hederas can be

5

purposely grown up trees with good effect, but again do prune *once a year* because if they are allowed to grow unchecked, the ivy becomes so heavy that the tree can no longer support it and a high wind or heavy snowfall can cause uprooting.

The *Hedera* species most widely cultivated in Britain are *H. canariensis, H. colchica,* and *H. helix.* The latter is our native ivy and has the greatest number of cultivars because of its ability to 'sport' in cultivation. 'Sport' is the term given to the production of a shoot different in character from the typical growth of the parent plant. It no doubt sports readily in the wild but I have not actually noticed this. A walk along an ivy-lined country lane would illustrate the point I think. Recently, when in a remote part of the Cotswolds I took specimens of ten different ivies growing on a low limestone wall in a stretch of about one hundred yards. I do not think they could all have been seedlings, indeed there were no adult plants around for them to have come from. I could have matched several with illustrations of some of the earliest named cultivars, and collection from the wild was no doubt the source of supply in the early days of growing ivies.

In spite of popular belief, ivy leaves in small quantities are not poisonous to animals. Ruminants particularly like ivy, as do horses, though milking animals should not be allowed to eat it, as it quickly taints the milk. The berries do not ripen until mid-winter and are an essential food source for birds when times are hard. The foliage of the adult forms of ivy is the breeding ground of moths and insects and also the nesting places of some of our larger birds such as owls, doves and pigeons.

Ivies are very adaptable—their ability to survive and even thrive in practically every climatic condition and almost any type of soil make them a very easy and useful plant to grow. The great gardeners in Britain and on the continent in the latter half of the nineteenth and early twentieth century realised this and used ivy extensively on a grand scale in the large gardens of those days. With the exacting skills that they applied in garden craft coupled with an abundance of trained labour, plants were grown to perfection. The contemporary garden literature is a curious mixture of praise (even causing literary head gardeners, who surely must have been very formidable gentlemen!, to wax lyrical in many an article) and fury about the damage ivy caused to walls and trees.

Shirley Hibberd is the best known author, and wrote one of the standard reference works on ivies—*The Ivy, its History, Uses and Characteristics* (1872). Many ivies grown then are listed in this book, and in other descriptive lists and contemporary catalogues. Many of the plants are still grown to-day under Hibberd's names, but it is not always the case, and even in modern times names sometimes get attached to the wrong plant. Therefore until an International Register of *Hedera* cultivars is published there is likely to be some disagreement about certain names. In

6

the list on pp.18-38 we have quoted alternative names that may be used for certain cultivars where we know about them.

Fig. 3. A corner of a town garden showing ivy used as ground cover, and trained up the base of a tree trunk.

7

2. Uses and cultivation

Ivies were the favourite houseplant in Victorian times but were arranged more in the style of room decoration than in the way we display houseplants today. Archways in rooms would have ivy trained to grow up and over them and windows would have ivy trained round the framing. Plants were also used for screening in large rooms and in summer empty fire places had ivy growing profusely in them. They thrived well in the erratic heating conditions of Victorian homes where other plants suffered in the fluctuating temperatures, and this is no doubt the reason why they enjoyed a long period of popularity. Today we use ivies as house plants again although mainly as small plants which is a pity because they are so easy to grow into handsome specimen plants which would be more reliable than some of the exotic plants we try to grow in our homes. We have only to heed the main instruction the Victorians left us which was "grow well and prune regularly". All varieties will grow inside as houseplants, but if the position is on the dark side then the green-leaved varieties are best.

Fig. 4. Ivy grown in a basket, allowing it to trail.

8

Fig. 5. An ivy-covered wall at Hidcote.

Ivy as a garden plant is used on a smaller scale than in the 19th century and this is to be regretted, as today's gardeners are overlooking a plant that enhances many a situation, in addition to remaining in foliage all the year round and needing very little attention. We have many cultivars available to-day, which are very superior in form and habit to the old varieties. They can be used for ground cover, growing up walls, filling in open fences, covering tree stumps, growing on awkward banks, in all the year round hanging baskets, as permanent trailing foliage for window boxes, growing up single supports as specimen feature plants and edging borders—the ivy's versatility is endless. Happily garden architects both here and on the continent are using *Hedera* more and more in their planting schemes. In Europe modern buildings are being clothed in ivy to reduce the stark effect of concrete and brick, and in doing so it has been found that it is also an effective natural insulating medium, keeping walls dry and warm, a fact well known to the Victorians.

Hederas will grow in a wide range of soils so long as they have enough water and the nutrient content is not too poor. *Hedera helix,* I know, grows better in an alkaline soil (which may be why it enjoys growing on walls), and I recommend applying a little lime before planting on acid soils. Cultivars of *Hedera colchica* and *H. canariensis* seem to prefer a neutral to acid soil and this is possibly why they do so well as house plants, grown in the soilless composts used to-day.

Figs. 6 & 7.
Two examples of ivy used as edging to a border

The green-leaved ivies will grow in sun or shade, but the leaves of some variegated ones may become scorched in bright sunlight and are usually better planted where they can get some shade for part of the day.

Ivies used as ground cover will, when established, crowd out most weeds and the growth is so resilient that walking on it, in moderation, will cause no damage. As with all ground covers the spacing at planting will depend on the final spread of the plant. An average spacing is about 30 inches (75 cm) apart, but staggered. Smaller, short-jointed plants such as 'Très Coupé' will be planted more closely, but vigorous plants will need more room.

Used on a wall or as fence covering, ivies really give an outstanding performance. An ugly fence or stark wall can be transformed by planting a selection of varieties or by using all one variety. Interspacing green varieties with the variegated makes an interesting as well as attractive feature and of course is good-looking all the year round. Plant out at about 1 yard (0.9 m) apart and when they grow they will eventually fill right in. The first year the plants will not seem to do much but once the stems begin to cling of their own accord, they will advance rapidly. To facilitate this, shoots can be attached to fences made of wood by nailing and tying. To encourage quick attachment to a brick wall paint the area where the plant will first make contact with the wall with a slurry of cow manure and water. Next tie the vines to short canes which have been inserted into the ground at an angle so that the top of the cane is touching the painted wall. This will guide them and hold them in the position in which you want them to grow. In the first year water the plants as often as necessary, especially if the weather is dry. Once they have become attached to their supports dryness does not seem to affect them at all. Ivies growing up walls or fences do not normally need watering once they have become established.

On January 24, 1860, *The Cottage Gardener and Country Gentleman* carried the following instructions for growing hederas up a wall. "Any Ivy wall to be the model of perfection every inch of it must be covered with ivy and not one leaf to shade another or to be farther from the wall than another and be as free from dead leaves and litter as the lawn in front of the drawing-room windows. Also birds are never allowed to make nests in models of this kind. The first thing to do covering an unsightly wall with ivy quickly is a thorough good rich deep dug border well drained. The better the border the faster the ivy will cover it. Any wall under ten feet high may be covered in one season and a half by planting ivy from seven to ten feet high out of pots about two feet apart. We have done so nearly four years back and by the middle of the second season every brick was covered; but for a higher wall we would use stronger dwarf plants and put them out in about April at one foot apart and water them with liquid manure in summer for the first two or three years. No plant we know will pay better for heavy watering and with the garden engine to dash water among the leaves. When once the wall is covered the labour and care begins. The knife, the eye, the hand and thé brain must go in harmony to "keep" the ivy as short as the lawn. No shoot is allowed to get one inch from the wall; and like seedlings the shoots must be thinned where too close and so must the leaves. Also the very long and the very short stalked ones, but there is not one of a thousand takes such a pride in ivy as to make a model of it." What is there left to say after this elaboration which covers each step so explicitly?

Fig. 8. A wall thickly covered with ivy.

Hederas can be used in the garden to cover arches and for growing up posts as free standing specimen plants—both very effective methods of display. To attain the latter drive an eight foot pointed post treated with wood preservative into the ground, then plant the chosen variety against it. Tie the trails upwards around the post and as the shoots grow, continue to tie into the post until the top is reached, then take out all growing tips. This will cause the plant to thicken out. When the column

12

Fig. 9. Ivy growing up pillars.

Fig. 10. Hedera colchica 'Dentata Variegata' in a tub.

13

has thickened, regularly clip back all over and this will keep the plant covered in juvenile growth. The variety 'Buttercup' is particularly suitable for this purpose if the situation is in full sun and the soil is limey; I know of a superb plant grown in this manner in the city of Bath. Not only is it planted in very limey soil but it is also growing in close proximity to a limestone wall and it is near a street lamp which remains alight all night. This plant, even in the mid-winter, is a beautiful golden yellow.

Another situation where ivy's natural inclinations can be used advantageously is by planting it closely on awkward banks instead of using grass which needs regular cutting. When established it will retain the soil and except for a yearly trim, will obviate the need for using a grass cutter at an awkward and often dangerous angle and will, by selecting attractive varieties, look much better than grass. Many green cultivars change colour when the cold weather comes, they turn varying shades of copper, purple and black and look splendid. They remain like this all winter and when the spring comes fade back to their normal green.

Hederas in hanging baskets are very good, for it means that one can have an effective basket all the year instead of just during the summer. A large basket, at least 12 inches (30 cm) diameter, which takes a good quantity of compost is best as the plants are to remain there for several years. Line with moss in the usual way and using John Innes potting compost No. 2 which is the most suitable type, plant up with five small bushy plants arranged all over the top of the basket. When the plants are growing well, pinch out the growing tips to encourage dense growth. Small and medium close-leafed varieties are the best ones to use and one variety only to a basket looks the most effective. It helps if, after the basket is planted up, it is left on the ground in a protected corner out of the wind and is watered regularly for about three months before hanging up. By then the plants will have rooted well into the compost and will not get loosened in the wind. After the first year, in the spring and summer, regular feeds of liquid fertiliser are beneficial. Once a year in the early spring, shorten the trails and don't forget to water if there is a prolonged dry spell.

Window boxes can be greatly enhanced by planting the front of the box with a row of small ivies. Left there permanently they will eventually form a thick cascade. Fewer bedding plants will be needed to fill up the box behind, when they are renewed each season.

3. Propagation

Propagation of ivies in their juvenile forms is usually easy as there are nearly always roots present somewhere on the stems, ready to grow into a root substrate. The recommended times for taking cuttings are in the

14

Fig. 11. Ivy used to good effect in a windowbox.

Fig. 12. Ivy providing a dense covering for a cottage wall.

autumn when rooting them outdoors, and in winter under glass, but they can be taken at almost any time of the year.

For rooting under glass, take shoots from the ends of the branches about 3 inches (7.5 cm) long, trimming the base to the joint (where a leaf joins the stem) or a little below. Insert two cuttings into a 3-inch pot of John Innes potting compost No. 1, or into a peat-based compost. To save space more cuttings can be inserted into a larger pot, but amateur gardeners do not usually need to propagate on such a scale. Place the pot into a plastic bag, tying the top up to a short cane inserted into the middle of the pot, so making a tent-like structure. This surrounds the cuttings with a moist, stable environment which encourages them to root quickly. Stand the pot in a warm place in the greenhouse or on a windowsill. When rooted (which will be after 4 to 6 weeks) shake out the cuttings separately and plant them into pots of John Innes potting No. 2 or soilless compost for potting. One young plant can be put into a 3-inch (7.5 cm) pot, or two into a $3\frac{1}{2}$-inch (9 cm) pot. When the plant(s) have become established they can be prepared for planting out in spring, by getting them gradually used to cooler conditions than in the greenhouse. If the plant is to be grown as a pot plant it can be potted on gradually into larger pots (and staked for support) using John Innes No. 2.

Ivies at the adult stage are usually difficult to root; even when they root they continue to produce adult foliage and do not revert to the juvenile stage again.

4. Troubles

Hederas are relatively pest free but they can be damaged by three sap feeding pests, namely soft scale, red spider mite and aphids. These pests thrive in hot dry conditions and are mainly found on plants in the greenhouse although ivies grown against warm walls may also be attacked.

Soft scale is a flat, oval, pale yellow or brown insect that can be found on the underside of the foliage, usually next to a leaf vein. The scales grow up to $\frac{1}{6}$ inch (4 mm) long and they make the foliage sticky with their sugary excretion known as honeydew. A black sooty mould often grows on the upper leaf surface where the honeydew is deposited. Red spider mites, which are yellowish green and only just visible to the naked eye, also live on the underside of the leaves. They cause a fine speckled discoloration of the upper leaf surface and, in heavy infestations, the leaves may fall off and the plant becomes covered in a fine silken webbing which is produced by the mites. Aphids may check growth by sucking sap from the shoot tips and young leaves. They may be black or green in colour.

All of these pests can be controlled by spraying thoroughly with malathion or diazinon. Soft scale and red spider mite are persistent pests and several applications at two-week intervals may be necessary if the plant is

Fig. 13. Hedera colchica 'Dentata Variegata' covering a wall
Fig. 14. Hedera canariensis 'Variegata' growing up a wall
covered with wire trellis.

heavily infested. Damping down will help to control red spider mite under glass.

Frequent application of malathion is known to result in the development of a resistant strain of red spider which will not be controlled satisfactorily by malathion. One of the other remedies will then have to be used. In order to delay the build-up of a resistant population of mites different pesticides should be used in rotation or else biological control may be tried (when a colony of a mite predator is introduced into the greenhouse to feed on the red spider mites).

Diseases are so rare that little needs to be said. On plants under glass a bacterial leaf spot may occur, and a *Septoria* root rot is also known.

5. Ivies to Grow

As with many other garden plants where large numbers of varieties are or have been grown, the naming of ivies is somewhat confused. The following list of names is of plants generally available from nurseries in Britain, under those names, so British gardeners should be able to buy them quite easily. These names do not always agree with the names given in the preliminary checklist of *Hedera helix* cultivars produced by the American Ivy Society in 1975, but we have noted any differences where they occur. There was recently a trial of ivies at the R.H.S. Garden at Wisley, where two hundred entries were grown together. Some of the confusion was sorted out when this trial was judged and evaluated. Synonyms of the varieties are given in parentheses. Unless qualified, specimen plants can be grown indoors or outdoors.

1. HEDERA CANARIENSIS. Strong growing variety with large shiny dark green ovate leaves and shiny wine-red stems. In winter these leaves are shaded copper. (Walls, fences: specimen plants).

Aurea Maculata (Margino-maculata). Large ovate cream and green marbled and spotted leaves with shiny red stems. Grow in light sunny position. (Walls, fences: specimen plants).

Azorica. Large matt green leaves with five to seven blunt lobes. Grows vigorously upright.

Variegata (Gloire de Marengo). Leaves irregularly marked dark green in the centre merging into silver grey and bordered with white. Shiny wine-red stems. (Walls, fences: specimen plants).

2. HEDERA COLCHICA. Persian Ivy. This ivy has the largest leaves of any ivy in the genus. They are dark matt green, ovate or elliptic, thick leathery leaves with red brown stems. Vigorous grower. Suitable for growing up walls or fences, as ground cover or as specimen plants indoors and out.

Dentata. Large, mid green, ovate, leathery leaves often slightly toothed, red brown stems. Vigorous grower. (Walls, fences: specimen plants).

Dentata Variegata. Large variegated yellow-cream and green leathery

Luzii

Marmorata Minor

Goldchild

Pointer

Curly Locks

Adam

Heron

Sulphur Heart

Cavendishii

Harald

Fig. 15. Hedera helix 'Green Ripple'.

Fig. 16. Hedera helix, the common ivy found wild in this country.

Fig. 17. Hedera helix 'Adam'.

leaves, ovate to elliptic in shape with green to red brown stems. (Walls, fences: specimen plants).

Sulphur Heart. (Paddy's Pride). Large ovate leathery leaves marked by an irregular yellow splash in the centre of leaf shading into pale green and then irregularly bordered dark green. (Walls, fences: specimen plant).

3. HEDERA HELIX. English ivy; common ivy. Very versatile and adaptable. It is found in Europe, Asia Minor and north Persia. Juvenile leaves are three to five lobed white, the adult foliage is ovate to rhomboidal. Nearly all our wild ivy is this type. (Ground cover: walls, fences).

Adam. Small silver variegated leaves that turn pink at edges in cold weather. Bushy growth. Highly recommended variety. (Walls, hanging baskets, window boxes: specimen plants).

Alt Heidelberg. Short-jointed compact plant with bluntly lanceolate leaves which sometimes have a small point appearing on one or both sides. The form of the leaves is rather variable. As the plant ages it throws out strong growing vining shoots of different character entirely. These are best removed to keep the original form true to type. (Rock garden or houseplant).

Angularis Aurea. Three to five lobed medium leaves. New foliage yellow, older foliage mottled green which turns chocolate brown in cold

24

weather. (Walls, fences, ground cover: specimen plants outside only as this variety needs to be grown in full sun).
Ardingly. Small silver variegated leaf tinged pink on edges in cold weather. Distinct from Adam. Neat, bushy habit. (Hanging basket, window boxes: specimen plants).
Atropurpurea. The small medium-sized leaf is oblong with a blunt point, at the terminal end two overlapping basal lobes. It is a very dull dark green which changes to blackish purple as soon as the weather becomes cold. A rather sparse grower, it is nevertheless very attractive when grown on a wall or fence in an exposed cold position.
Bodil. White, yellow and green spotted and blotched, five-pointed leaves. (Hanging baskets, walls, fences).
Brokamp. Dark green leathery lanceolate and deltoid medium sized leaves. Strong growing dense habit. Turns to lovely copper shades in cold weather. (Walls, fences, hanging baskets, window boxes, ground cover).
Buttercup. Yellow green leaves. New growth bright golden yellow which will remain this colour if grown in correct conditions. (See p.14.)

Fig. 18. Hedera helix 'Chicago Variegated'.

25

Caecilia. The medium sized tri-lobed green-edged cream leaves have very curly edges giving them an attractive frilled appearance. Vining habit. (Walls, fences, hanging baskets, houseplants).

Caenwoodiana (Grey Arrow). Grey green narrow leaves five lobed, the centre lobe being the longest and the lateral lobes much shorter, heavy white veins down the centre. Stiff upright grower. (Walls, fences: specimen plants). (See also Pedata Heron).

Cavendishii (Tricolor, Sheen Silver). Triangular ovate leaves of a whitey silver variegation. Medium small sized leaves, slow grower but eventually makes a handsome plant. (Walls, fences: specimen plants). Grows better outside.

Chicago. Green, small to medium-sized, three to five lobed, soft textured leaves. Vigorous grower. (Walls, fences: ground cover).

Chicago Variegated. Green and cream variegated version of Chicago. (Walls, fences: hanging baskets, window boxes: specimen plants).

Congesta. Stiffly erect shoots crowded on the stems, with triangularly-shaped, cupped leaves. (Rock garden or over a tree stump). Does not cling. Often confused with 'Conglomerata'.

Fig. 19. Hedera helix 'Congesta'.

26

Conglomerata. A slow growing, stiff-stemmed variety with blunt lobed thick leathery leaves. The plant remains low growing. (Rock garden or over a tree stump or low wall). Does not cling.

Conglomerata Erecta. Blunt-lobed, leathery leaves growing on thick, curved stems. This variety looks like 'Conglomerata' but grows in a more upright fashion and makes a much taller plant. Does not cling.

Crippsii. Small leathery cream and green variegated leaves. Very slow grower.

Cristata. (Parsley Crested). Pale shiny green, round leathery medium-sized leaves, twisted and crimped on edges. The leaves turn beautifully red all over on underside and blotched red on top during cold weather. Vigorous grower. (Walls, fences, hanging baskets, ground cover: specimen plants).

Curly Locks. See Manda's Crested.

Deltoidea. Bluntly deltoid, dark green, thick leathery leaves with two basal lobes which often overlap. The leaves turn a purplish bronze in cold weather. Stiff thick stems. (Good shaped specimen: walls, fences).

Digitata. Is one of three varieties that often get confused. It is easily distinguished from the other two, 'Palmata' and 'Gracilis', by its more digitate outline and its dark green colour with the veins showing prominently. It also has the largest leaf. (Walls, fences: specimen plants).

Fig. 20. Hedera helix 'Conglomerata'.

27

Erecta. See Russelliana.

Eva. Small green and cream leaves with forward pointing lobes attractively shaped and marked. Bushy grower. (Hanging baskets, window boxes; walls, fences: specimen plants).

Glacier. Small, medium greyish silver leaves, well marked, with distinctive red stems. Strong grower. A good all round variety that is suitable for any situation inside or outside.

Glymii (Tortuosa). Shiny dark green, mostly ovate, leathery medium leaves which turn very dark purple in cold weather. Young plants have a percentage of three-lobed leaves with a longer centre lobe. (Walls, fences, ground cover: specimen plants outside).

Goldchild. An attractive golden version of Chicago Variegated which was raised from a sport by Rochfords. It is a slow grower but well worth persevering with as it is most attractive. It is used mostly as a house plant because it grows so slowly but it can be grown successfully outside. (Hanging baskets, low wall: specimen plants).

Goldheart (Jubilee) (Oro di Bogliasco). Probably one of the most popu-

Fig. 21. Hedera helix 'Harald'.

28

lar cultivars in this country, it is reputed to have come from Italy. It has a small, neat, three to five pointed green leaf with a golden yellow centre and reddish stems. It is a slow growing plant to start off with and grows best up a wall as once it can attach itself to brick or stone it gets away quickly and the leaf colouring and markings show at their best. If grown in acid soil green shoots are inclined to appear in the plant. These should be cut out and some lime worked in around the roots. (Walls, fences: specimen plants). This variety will also retain its yellow colouring even if it is not grown in full sunlight.

Gracilis. Small green leaves, three to five pointed lobes and red stems with a wiry habit. All the foliage turns a lovely wine colour at the first sign of cold weather. (Walls, fences, ground cover: specimen plants).

Green Ripple. Medium, dark green, leathery, jaggedly lobed leaves, the centre lobe being the longest. Vigorous grower. Changes to a nice copper colour in cold weather. Suitable for every situation inside or outside.

Hamilton. Large distinctly five cuspid lobed mid-green leaves of leathery texture. Strong growing stems. This plant, if supported by a stake, has a very good architectural form. Collected by me as a sport from 'Hibernica'. (Specimen plant outside or houseplant).

Harald. Medium green and yellow variegated shiny leaves paling to

Fig. 22. Adult form of Hedera helix 'Goldheart'.

29

Fig. 23. A specimen plant of Hedera helix 'Congesta' in the garden.

cream as leaf ages. Vigorous grower suitable in all conditions.
Hazel. Creamy white leaves speckled and marbled green. Raised by Rochfords from a sport of 'Adam'. Suitable for hanging baskets, or as a specimen plant indoors chiefly as it seems to need dull conditions for its leaf pattern to show to best advantage.
Heise. Another attractive silver leaf, very bushy vigorous grower with larger leaves than 'Adam'. Suitable for every situation inside or outside.
Hibernica (Irish ivy). Dark green shiny medium sized, five lobed leaves. Vigorous grower. (Walls, fences, ground cover).
Hibernica Pallida. Dark green, blunt, five lobed shiny leaf, mottled cream. (Walls, fences, ground cover: specimen plants).
Ivalace. Small, five-lobed, dark green leathery leaves with upcurled margins, leaves change to a coppery shade during cold weather. Grows densely. Suitable for all situations inside or outside.
Kolibri. Small grey green and white leaves irregularly splashed with shiny dark green blotches. (Houseplants).
Little Diamond. Small medium-sized, silver variegated leaf which is diamond shaped on young trails. Grows in a distinctive style. Dense foliage on stems which branch stiffly outwards when growing upright and in a flat circular fashion if growing on the ground or in a hanging basket. (Hanging baskets: specimen plants).
Luzii (Lutzii). Small light gold leaf blotched and marbled green. Suitable for all situations inside or outside.
Manda's Crested (Curly Locks). Medium sized, soft pale green wavy

Fig. 24. Hedera helix 'Bodil'.

31

Fig. 25. A tub containing hostas and ivy. The pleasing line and graceful form of the ivy softens the definite outline of the concrete container.

five-pointed leaves which turn a beautiful red pink on undersides and blotched red on surface during cold weather. This variety makes superb hanging baskets and good specimen plants and is suitable for growing up walls and fences.

Marginata Major. Medium green, triangular ovate leaves. Centre grey-green shaded mid green with cream margins. (Walls, fences: specimen plants).

Marmorata Minor (Discolor, Minor Marmorata). Small green leaf speckled and blotched dark green. (Walls, fences: specimen plants).

Meagheri. Small green three-lobed leaves which in the young state remain very slim. As the foliage ages the leaves take on a wider form and can be confused with 'Shamrock', the difference being that 'Shamrock' grows thick and bushy all the time whereas 'Meagheri' grows long thin trails which need to be trimmed causing the plant to thicken up. (Walls, fences, hanging baskets, window boxes).

Minima (Spetchley). Tiny dark green leaves, mostly three lobed,

Fig. 26. Hedera helix 'Luzii'.

33

sometimes five, changing to copper colour in winter. Will cover a rock or wall with quite dense minute leaves and so is ideal for the rock garden.
Nymans. Dull, dark green, five lobed leaf, the centre V-shaped lobe being half the length of the whole leaf with two small side lobes and two prominent basal lobes. In summer the veins show up prominently white. (Walls, fences, ground cover, specimen plants).
Neilsonii (Neilson). Small, bright green, five lobed leaf, the centre pointed lobe being the longest and the side lobes, though small, also pointed. Bushy habit, the vines will attain a good height but are slow to do so. Changes to red coppery shades in cold weather. Suitable for all situations inside and out.
Palmata. Green, palmately lobed, small to medium-sized leaves. Quite distinct from 'Gracilis' and 'Digitata' (see Fig. 31) and in cold weather even more so when the leaves take on their brown red winter colouring. (Walls, fences, ground cover: specimen plants).
Pedata Heron (Heron). It is known as the Heron's Foot ivy. It has five bright green pedately lobed leaves with white raised veins sparsely

Fig. 27. Hedera helix 'Sagittaefolia'.

34

arranged on the stems. Can be confused with 'Caenwoodiana' as they are very similar. (Walls, fences: specimen plants).

Pittsburgh. Bright green, five lobed medium leaf which changes to a most attractive copper shade in cold weather. Vigorous grower. Suitable in all situations outside.

Plume d'Or. Very small, narrow, pedately lobed green leaves growing in a crowded fashion on the stems. Thick bushy overall growth with short thick golden-green shoots springing out all over the plant. (Hanging baskets, window boxes, ground cover).

poetica *(chrysocarpa)*. Bright green, medium sized shallowly-lobed leaves. Stiff upright grower. (Walls: specimen plants).

Pointer. See Professor F. Tobler.

Professor F. Tobler (Pointer). Green, narrow, single lobed leaves growing in clusters of three closely along the stems. Bushy habit and vigorous grower. Turns a copper shade in cold weather. (Hanging baskets, window boxes, ground cover: specimen plants). This plant is also known in the U.K. as 'Pedley's Green Finger' and 'Finger Post'.

Russelliana. (Erecta). Dark green, leathery, medium-sized ovate leaves which grow in a cupped manner at the basal end while the blunt point grows in the normal way which gives the leaf an attractive curl. The distinctive feature of this plant is the perpendicular stiff stems which grow from the base of the plant with all the leaves arranged in a stiff precise manner to the tip of the stem. The leaves at the lower end of the plant are always twice as large as the leaves at the top of the plant. This variety makes an attractive feature plant with little support and is therefore chiefly grown as a specimen plant inside or outside.

Sagittaefolia. This is one of the varieties with which there is some confusion in name. The original plant of this name was, according to Hibberd, "usually bluntly three lobed, the centre lobe projecting forward in the form of the letter "V"". Although this plant is still in cultivation it is not the plant that is sold in this country as 'Sagittaefolia'. The plant used extensively here has a light green, slender, five lobed leaf, the centre narrow point nearly twice as long as it is broad with two pointed side lobes and two pointed base lobes. The plant makes a lot of shoots which gives a dense habit and it is a fast grower. Suitable in all conditions inside or outside. On the continent this variety is known as 'Königer's Auslese', which without a doubt is the correct name.

Sagittaefolia Variegata. This is the cream and green variegated version of the previous variety and is the universally accepted legitimate name for this plant in spite of the confusion over the name of its green relative. It is extremely attractive and can be used in every situation except ground cover. Also known as 'Königer's Variegated'.

Shamrock. Has a small, green, three lobed leaf. The side lobes are bent forward making the leaf appear cupped. The side lobes are sometimes toothed which on an older leaf develops into small basal lobes. The plant has a dense habit and turns a good copper shade in cold weather. It is suitable for flat growing situations such as hanging baskets, window boxes and ground cover or low growing specimen plants inside or outside.

Spectabilis Aurea. A very attractive gold blotched arborescent form of ivy. This variety is in short supply as it is very slow to root. There is a beautiful specimen to be seen growing on the wall of an hotel at Church Stretton in Shropshire and another on a hotel at Dunchurch, Warwickshire. Both are at their most brilliant in the summer months. (Walls: specimen plant outside only).

Spectre. This is a green and cream variegated sport from 'Triton'. Suitable for hanging baskets or any low situation as it is a slow grower, inside or outside.

Stuttgart. Medium green five lobed leaf, slightly wavy dense habit. A sport from 'Ivalace'. (Ground cover, hanging baskets).

Très Coupé. Very small, narrow, five lobed leaf with long pointed centre lobe and small pointed side and basal lobes. Very bushy habit and rather slow growing. (Low walls, fences, ground cover, hanging baskets,

Fig. 28. Hedera helix 'Sagittaefolia Variegata'.

36

Fig. 29. Ivy planted to cover an old tree stump.

window boxes: specimen plants). It is a sport from 'Sagittaefolia'.
Trinity. A very unusual and attractive variety. There is always a mixture
of three different coloured leaves, dark green, mottled white and green,
and off white with green veins. The leaf has five lobes, the centre one

being the longest. Suitable in a sheltered situation outside; although the cold weather does not kill the plant, late frosts cause the white leaves to brown. It makes a very good house plant.

Triton (Green Feather). A very unusual leaf formation. Five slender lobes tapering to very fine points, the three centre ones being very long and often twisted. The texture is leathery and dark green in colour with prominent whitish veins. (Hanging baskets: specimen plants).

4. HEDERA NEPALENSIS (Himalayan ivy). Mid-green, shiny, ovate lanceolate leaves sometimes toothed and occasionally with basal lobes. (Walls, fences: specimen plants).

5. HEDERA RHOMBEA. Japanese ivy has rather a delicate appearance, though quite hardy in this country. Green ovate leaves, often heart-shaped at the base, which are sometimes slightly lobed. (Walls, fences, ground cover).

Variegata. As above with a narrow white margin to the leaves. (Walls, fences).

Fig. 30. An example of mixed planting in a trough in a town garden. Note the attractive effect of the contrasting types of foliage.

38

Glossary

Basal	Of, at, or forming the base.
Crenate	Finely lobed.
Cuspid	Pointed end (esp. of leaf).
Deltoid	Broadly triangular.
Elliptic	Oval, with regularly rounded ends.
Entire	Undivided.
Lanceolate	Shaped like a spear-head, tapering to each end.
Ovate	Oval.
Rhomboidal	Shaped like a rhombus.
Undulate	Wavy (especially margins of leaves).

Fig. 31. Note the different leaf shapes of these three ivies which are frequently confused. Left, Hedera helix 'Palmata'; centre, H.h. 'Gracilis'; right, H.h. 'Digitata'.